Highlights
Hidden Pictures

Things That Go
Puzzles

HIGHLIGHTS PRESS
Honesdale, Pennsylvania

Welcome, Hidden Pictures Puzzlers!

Use your stickers on the black-and-white-puzzles to find the hidden objects.
When you finish a puzzle, check it off √. Good luck, and happy puzzling!

Contents

Cover art by Mitch Mortimer

Contents

Art by John Nez

Seaworthy Turtle

Mitten

Crown

Button

Boomerang

Comb

Golf Ball

Pencil

Cupcake

Snowman

Art by Patrick Girouard

6

Hogging the Tractor

Glove

Comb

Muffin

Apple

Sock

Eyeglasses

Dog Bone

Pencil

Art by David Coulson

7

Motorbike Race

GATE 12

A Choo-Choo Train

Sailboat

Piece of Popcorn

Dish

Wedge of Lemon

Ruler

Comb

Seashell

Flashlight

Race to the Stars

Art by Jamie Smith

Button

Crayon

Ice-Cream Bar

Candy Cane

Dog Bone

Jar

Horseshoe

Doughnut

Traffic

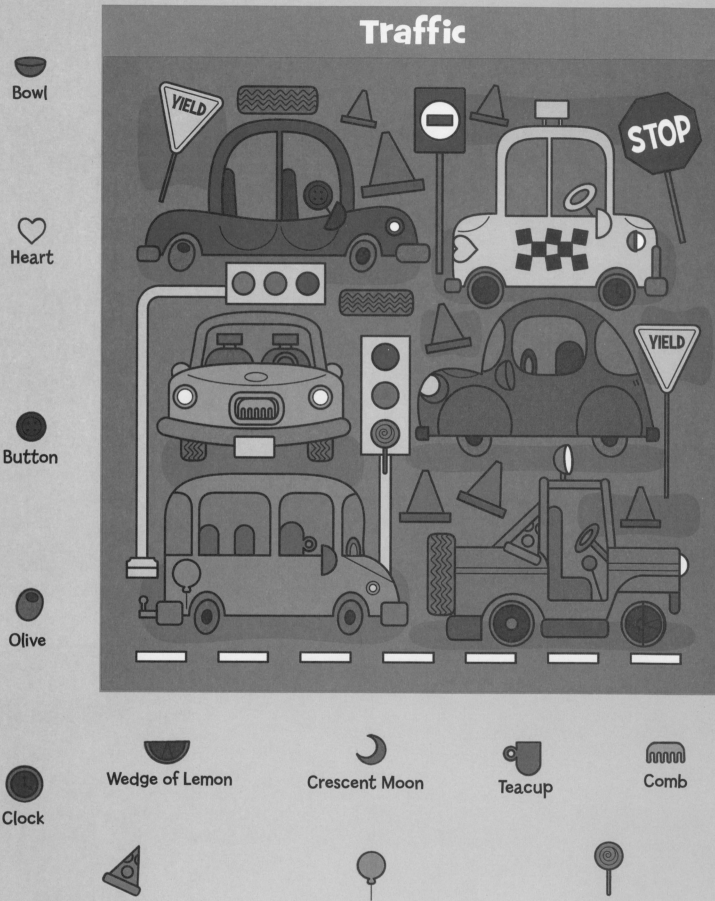

Bowl

Heart

Button

Olive

Clock

Wedge of Lemon

Crescent Moon

Teacup

Comb

Slice of Pizza

Balloon

Lollipop

Art by Steve Mack

Canoe Duo

Slice of Cake

Coin

Crayon

Candle

Can

Art by Kelly Kennedy

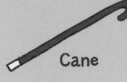
Cane

Cupcake

Comb

17

Biking by the Sea

Butterfly

Fork

Football

Seashell

Heart

Art by Diane Palmisciano

Worm

Pencil

Coat Hanger

Bear's First Canoe Trip

Broom

Flag

Apple

Sunglasses

Baseball Cap

Teacup

Sneaker

Cupcake

Art by Gillian Guile

SHARK

I BRAKE FOR REEFS

22

Fisherman's Ferry

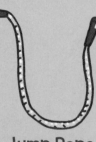

Paintbrush

Kite

Turtle

Lemon

Soccer Ball

Bow Tie

Jump Rope

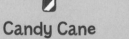

Candy Cane

Slice of Pie

Boot

Pencil

Boomerang

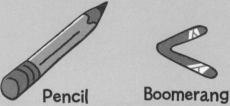

Art by Dave Klug

24

Car Tunes

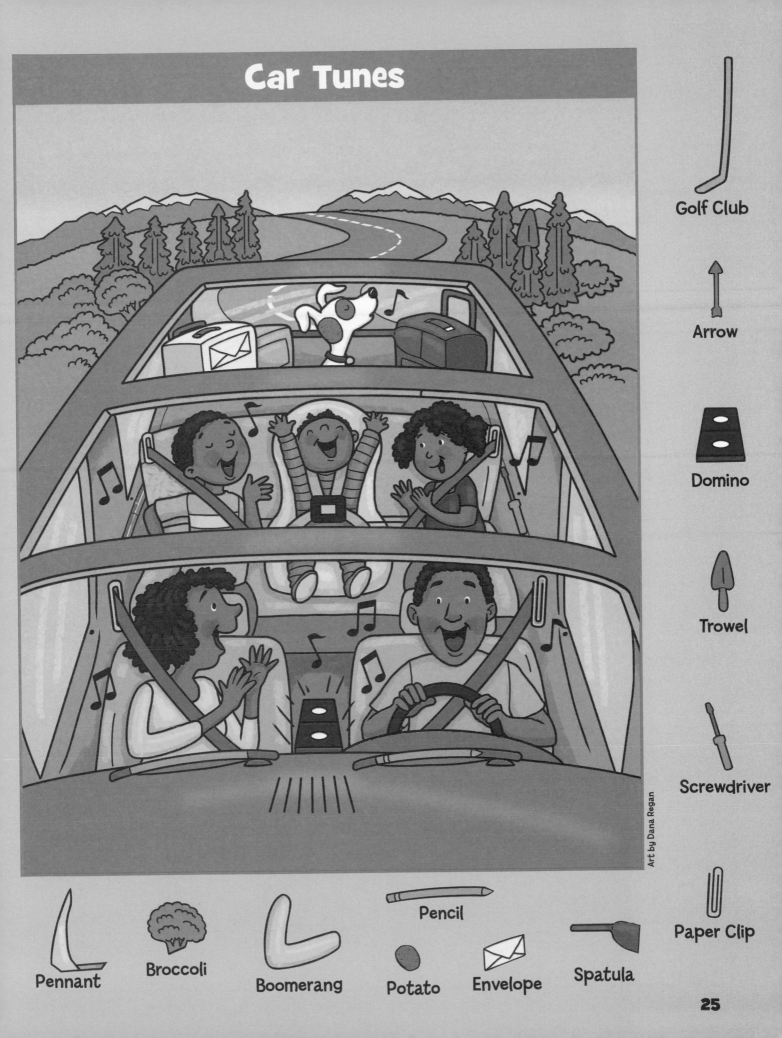

Golf Club

Arrow

Domino

Trowel

Screwdriver

Paper Clip

Pennant

Broccoli

Boomerang

Pencil

Potato

Envelope

Spatula

Art by Dana Regan

25

Snow Day

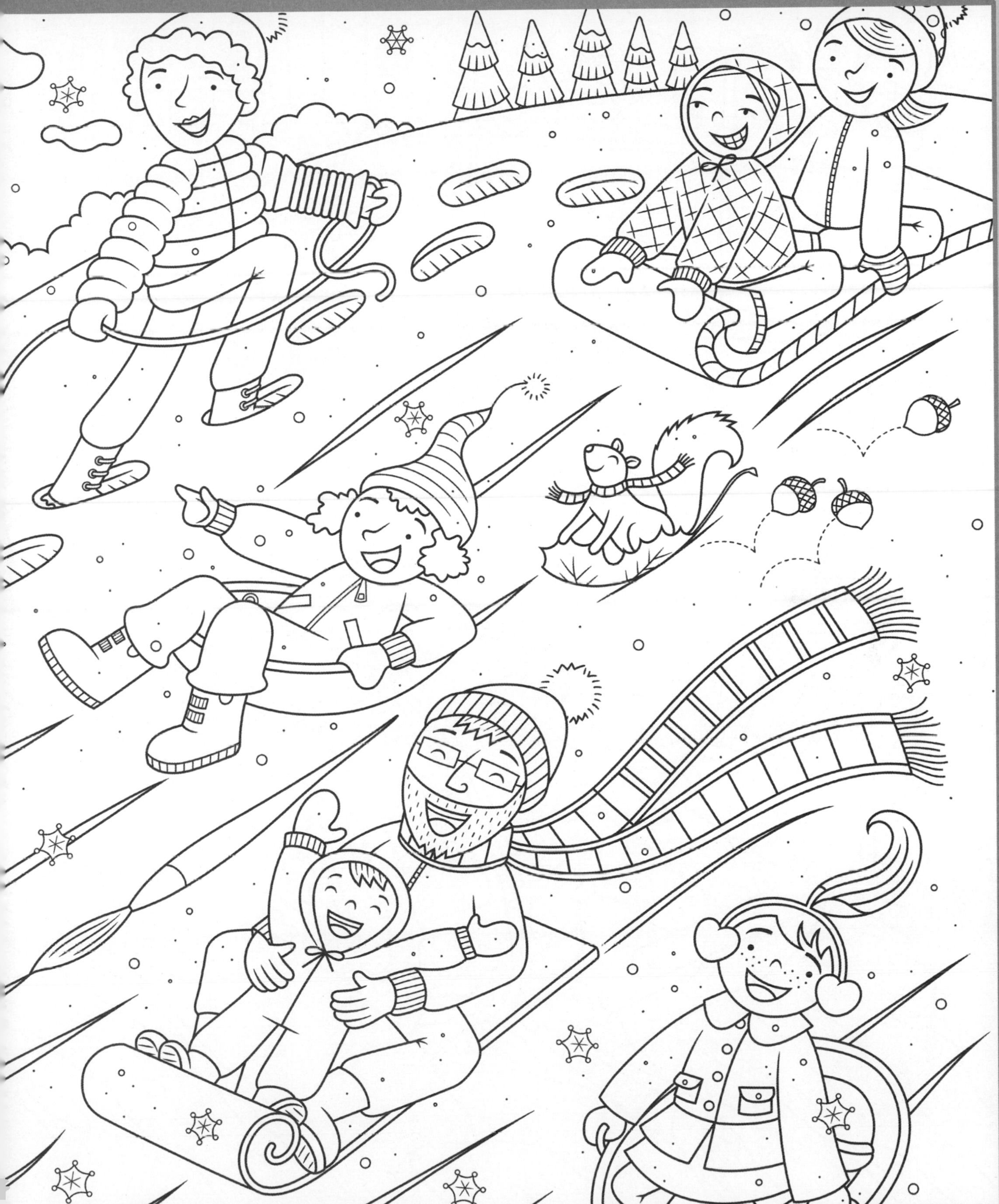

Art by Christine Schneider

The Turtle and the Hare

Slice of Bread

Pencil

Telescope

Crescent Moon

Fish

Bell

Horseshoe

Yo-Yo

Ferris Wheel

Fork

Flower

Flashlight

Flowerpot

Art by Kelly Kennedy

Four-Leaf Clover

Fish

Frying Pan

Football

Skateboard Park

Carrot

Key

Sock

Golf Club

Saltshaker

Scarf

Boomerang

Toothbrush

Wedge of Orange

Slice of Pizza

Art by Dave Klug

Raft Ride

Tennis Racket

Rocket Ship

Ruler

Rake

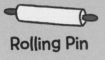
Rolling Pin

Scarf

Flower

Ring

Art by Kelly Kennedy

Construction Crew

Ice-Cream Cone

Book

Horn

Screwdriver

Pencil

Chicken

42

Doughnut

Heart

Eyeglasses

Ship

Hat

Spool of Thread

Shoe

Mitten

Art by Tim Davis

Up, Up, and Away

Stamp

Candy Cane

Sock

Hat

Art by Jim Paillot

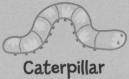
Caterpillar

Slice of Pizza

Horseshoe

Basketball

Two Wheels!

Stamp

Pear

Carrot

Lime

Bell

Cupcake

Slice of Pizza

Fish

Art by Mike Dammer

48

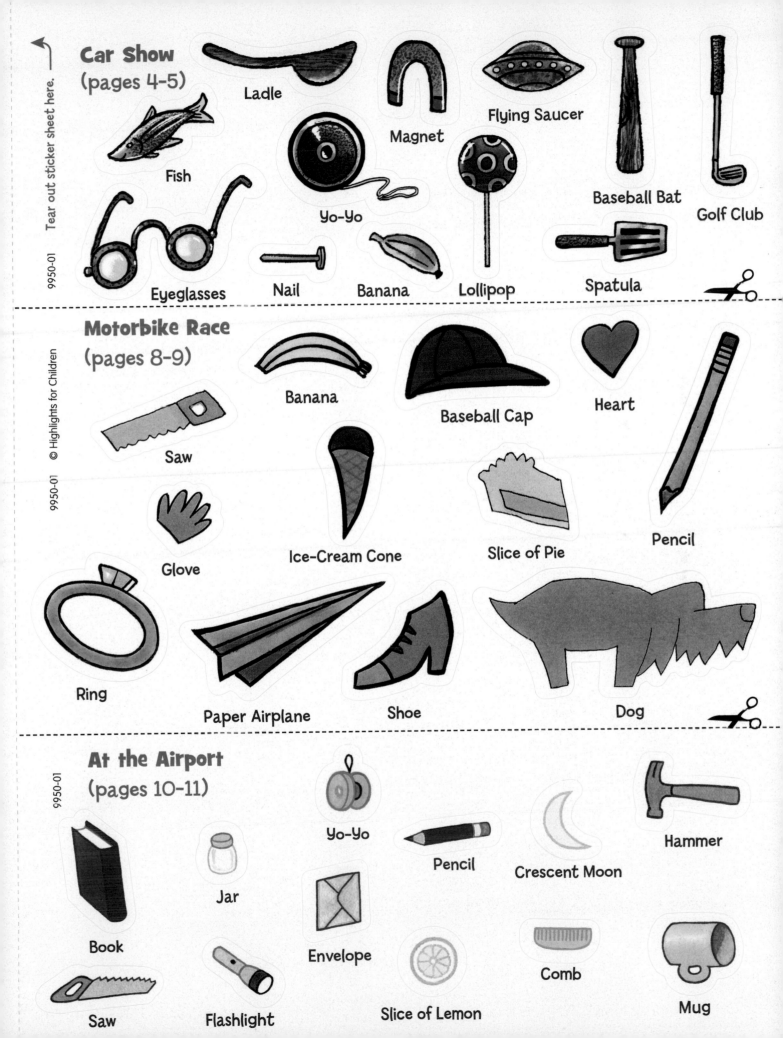

Car Show
(pages 4–5)

Ladle

Magnet

Flying Saucer

Baseball Bat

Golf Club

Fish

Yo-Yo

Eyeglasses

Nail

Banana

Lollipop

Spatula

Motorbike Race
(pages 8–9)

Banana

Baseball Cap

Heart

Saw

Ice-Cream Cone

Slice of Pie

Pencil

Glove

Ring

Paper Airplane

Shoe

Dog

At the Airport
(pages 10–11)

Yo-Yo

Pencil

Crescent Moon

Hammer

Book

Jar

Envelope

Comb

Saw

Flashlight

Slice of Lemon

Mug

Highlights

Hidden Pictures

Highlights

Hidden Pictures

Highlights

Hidden Pictures

Highlights

Hidden Pictures

Highlights

Hidden Pictures

Highlights

Hidden Pictures

Highlights

Raccoon's RV
(pages 16–17)

Book

Cherry

Leaf

Slice of Pie

Slice of Watermelon

Cinnamon Bun

Lime

Sun

Envelope

Frying Pan

Magnifying Glass

Whale

Submarine Life
(pages 20–21)

Wedge of Cheese

Mushroom

Broom

Cookie

Flag

Olive

Star

Candy Corn

Nail

Pen

Tack

Crayon

Bike Trail
(pages 22–23)

Teacup

Caterpillar

Slice of Pie

Saltshaker

Wedge of Lemon

Spoon

Celery

Wristwatch

Bell

Banana

Crayon

Feather

Highlights

Hidden Pictures

Highlights

Hidden Pictures

Highlights

Hidden Pictures

Highlights

Hidden Pictures

Highlights

Hidden Pictures

Highlights

Hidden Pictures

Highlights

Snow Day
(pages 26-27)

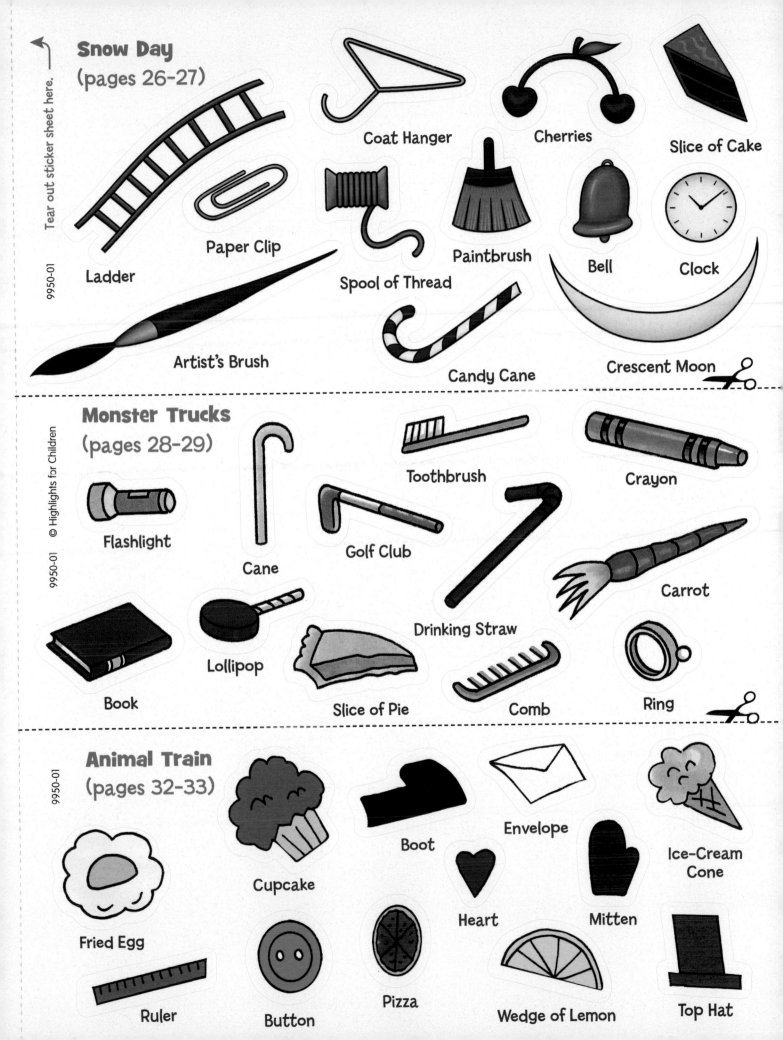

Coat Hanger

Cherries

Slice of Cake

Paper Clip

Spool of Thread

Paintbrush

Bell

Clock

Ladder

Artist's Brush

Candy Cane

Crescent Moon

Monster Trucks
(pages 28-29)

Toothbrush

Crayon

Flashlight

Cane

Golf Club

Carrot

Drinking Straw

Book

Lollipop

Slice of Pie

Comb

Ring

Animal Train
(pages 32-33)

Envelope

Boot

Ice-Cream Cone

Cupcake

Heart

Mitten

Fried Egg

Ruler

Button

Pizza

Wedge of Lemon

Top Hat

River Otter Rafters
(pages 34-35)

Tear out sticker sheet here.

9950-01

Glove

Scissors

Carrot

Handbell

Jug

Heart

Bat

Banana

Toothbrush

Teacup

Spoon

Rush Hour
(pages 38-39)

© Highlights for Children

9950-01

Envelope

Ring

Wristwatch

Sailboat

Book

Leaf

Sock

Slice of Pie

Cupcake

Pencil

Banana

Golf Club

Taking Flight
(pages 40-41)

9950-01

Teacup

Ice-Cream Cone

Cowboy Hat

Magnifying Glass

Thermos

Trowel

Wristwatch

Megaphone

Snail

Binder

Hot Dog

Sock

Glove

Doughnut

Iron

Kids' Car Wash
(pages 44-45)

Glove

Book

Ring

Mitten

Lollipop

Fork

Leaf

Wishbone

Drinking Straw

Saucepan

Waffle

Oar

Load Them Up
(pages 46-47)

Screwdriver

Envelope

Book

Toothbrush

Key

Comb

Ring

Tube of Toothpaste

Golf Club

Pencil

Mallet

Crescent Moon

Dog Drivers
(pages 50-51)

Saucepan

Candle

Tube of Toothpaste

Cracker

Cupcake

Heart

Needle

Mushroom

Boomerang

Ring

Button

Key

Candy Corn

Sneaker

Wishbone

Ruler

Tack

Flyswatter

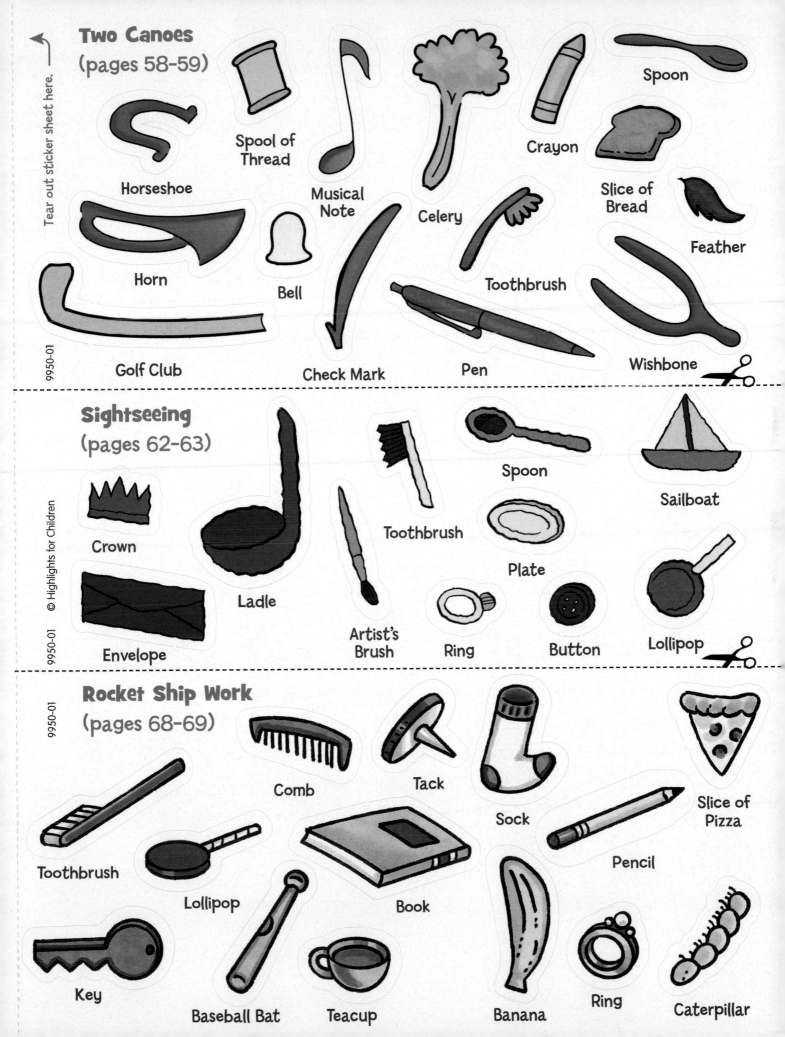

Two Canoes
(pages 58–59)

9950-01

Horseshoe

Spool of Thread

Musical Note

Celery

Crayon

Spoon

Slice of Bread

Feather

Horn

Bell

Toothbrush

Golf Club

Check Mark

Pen

Wishbone

Sightseeing
(pages 62–63)

9950-01

Crown

Ladle

Toothbrush

Spoon

Sailboat

Plate

Envelope

Artist's Brush

Ring

Button

Lollipop

Rocket Ship Work
(pages 68–69)

9950-01

Comb

Tack

Sock

Slice of Pizza

Pencil

Toothbrush

Lollipop

Book

Key

Baseball Bat

Teacup

Banana

Ring

Caterpillar

Highlights Highlights
Hidden Pictures Hidden Pictures
Highlights Highlights
Hidden Pictures Hidden Pictures
Highlights Highlights
Hidden Pictures Hidden Pictures
Highlights Highlights
Hidden Pictures Hidden Pictures
Highlights Highlights
Hidden Pictures Hidden Pictures
Highlights Highlights
Hidden Pictures Hidden Pictures
Highlights Highlights

Coasting
(pages 72-73)

Book

Leaf

Ladder

Ring

Slice of Pie

Button

Pencil

Golf Club

Sailboat

Envelope

Spatula

Spoon

Hot-Air Balloons
(pages 76-77)

Banana

Ladder

Doughnut

Boomerang

Eyeglasses

Matchstick

Paintbrush

Chef's Hat

Game Piece

Snake

T-Shirt

Horseshoe

Pencil

Tea Bag

Shuttlecock

Screwdriver

Adhesive Bandage

Comb

Horn

Zipper

Wash and Wax
(pages 82-83)

Envelope

Ring

Button

Lollipop

Slice of Pie

Bell

Ladle

Golf Club

Snake

Ice-Cream Cone

Ladder

Ruler

Crow in the Snow

Necktie

Acorn

Dart

Star

Heart

Car

Balloon

Pie

Art by Nathan Jarvis

53

Two Canoes

Animal Cars

Banana

Lollipop

Mushroom

Waffle

Bowling Ball

Snail

Ruler

Comb

Wedge of Orange

Pencil

Saucepan

Hammer

Art by Laura Huliska-Beith

Blast Off!

Baseball Bat

Ring

Basketball

Pencil

Boot

Magnifying Glass

Heart

Doughnut

Art by Kelly Kennedy

Queenie's Ride

Crayon

Comb

Sock

Football

Fork

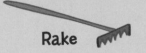
Rake

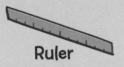
Ruler

Artist's Brush

Art by Dave Clegg

64

Sleigh Ride

Ladder

Lollipop

Snake

Lightning Bolt

Arrow

Toothbrush

Hockey Stick

Art by Jennifer Harney

Party Hat

Heart

Banana

Spool of Thread

Candy Cane

Pencil

Wheels on the Bus

Leaf

Pencil

Oar

Art by Jackie Stafford

Banana

 Sock

 Sailboat

 Heart

 Fish

River Rafting

Cotton Candy

Bird

Artist's Brush

Wishbone

Teacup

Sock

Golf Club

Spoon

Art by Neil Numberman

Around and Around

Toothbrush

Banana

Sock

Slice of Pizza

Art by Dave Klug

Balloon

Rake

Eyeglasses

Seashell

Shake Break

Pie

Guitar

Necktie

Potato

Purse

Sock

Star

Tomato

Art by Mike Moran

Paddle Boat

Domino

Teacup

Star

Fork

Rabbit

Scissors

Ruler

Skateboard

Art by Janet McDonnell

74

Train to City

Comb

Ruler

Slice of Pizza

Crescent Moon

Banana

Waffle

Ladder

Doughnut

Wedge of Lemon

Toothbrush

Artist's Brush

Domino

Art by Tamara Petrosino

City Cabs

Hockey Stick

Pencil

Ladder

Toothbrush

Iron

Thimble

Envelope

Acorn

Cupcake

Button

Ruler

Banana

Art by Neil Numberman

Ice Cream!

Iron

Igloo

Ice Skate

Ice Cube

Island

Art by Kelly Kennedy

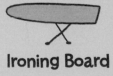
Ironing Board

Worm

Lizard

Friendly Fireman

Ice-Cream Bar

Flashlight

Ring

Spoon

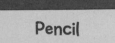
Pencil

Suitcase

Slice of Pizza

Stamp

Art by Mike Moran

80

Plane Ride

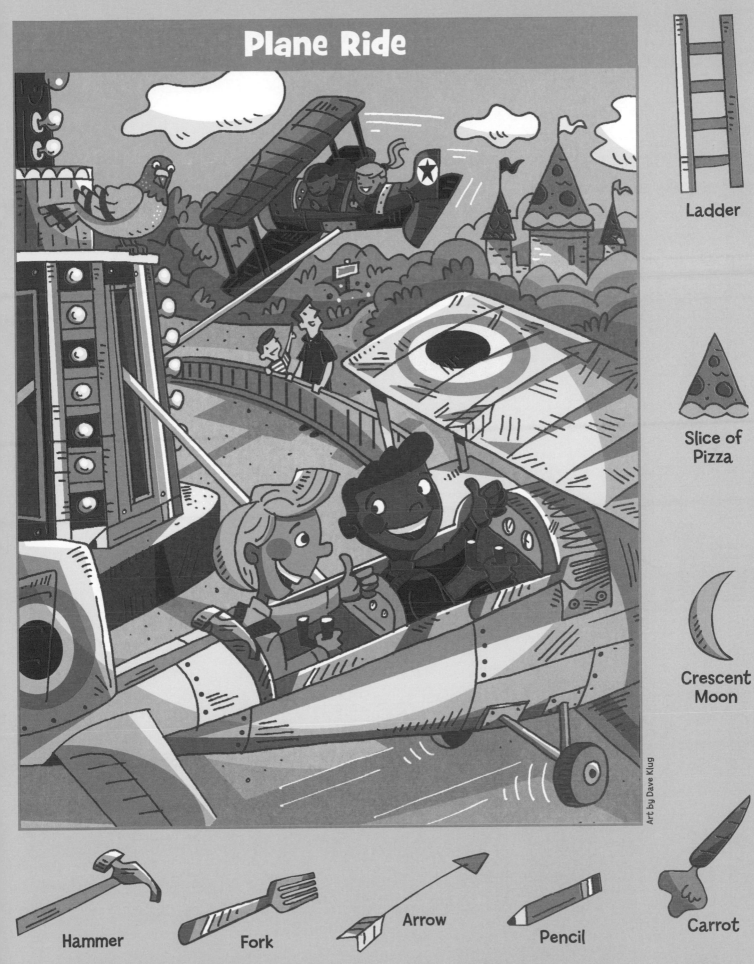

Ladder

Slice of Pizza

Crescent Moon

Hammer

Fork

Arrow

Pencil

Carrot

Art by Dave Klug

Lola's
CAR
WASH

Art by Dave Helton

Ice-Cream Truck

Slice of Pizza

Bat

Gavel

Party Hat

Flag

Muffin

Envelope

Fish

Candy Corn

Bell

Ruler

Olive

Broccoli

Slice of Watermelon

Crown

Art by Bill Golliher

84

Sailing Sights

Closed Umbrella

Ruler

Piece of Popcorn

Banana

Baseball

Button

Cookie

Hot Dog

Art by Laura Watson

Busy City

Flashlight

Megaphone

Sock

Crayon

Comb

Slice of Pizza

Boot

Lollipop

Art by Mary Sullivan

▼Pages 4-5

▼Page 6

▼Page 7

▼Pages 8-9

▼Pages 10-11

▼Page 12

Answers

▼ Page 13

▼ Page 14

▼ Page 15

▼ Pages 16–17

▼ Page 18

▼ Page 19

▼ Pages 20–21

▼Pages 22-23

▼Page 24

▼Page 25

▼Pages 26-27

▼Pages 28-29

▼Page 30

Answers

▼Page 31

▼Pages 32-33

▼Pages 34-35

▼Page 36

▼Page 37

▼Pages 38-39

▼ Pages 40-41

▼ Page 42

▼ Page 43

▼ Pages 44-45

▼ Pages 46-47

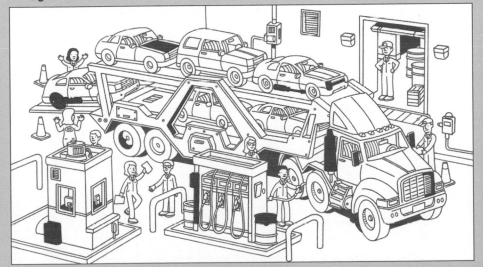

▼ Page 48

Answers

▼Page 49

▼Pages 50-51

▼Pages 52-53

▼Pages 54-55

▼Pages 56–57

▼Pages 58–59

▼Page 60

▼Page 61

▼Pages 62–63

Answers

▼Page 64

▼Page 65

▼Page 66

▼Page 67

▼Pages 68–69

▼Page 70

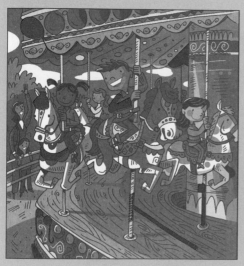

▼Page 71

▼Pages 72-73

▼Page 74

▼Page 75

▼Pages 76-77

▼Page 78

▼Page 79

▼Page 80

Answers

▼ Page 81

▼ Pages 82–83

▼ Page 84

▼ Page 85

▼ Page 86

Published by Highlights Press
815 Church Street
Honesdale, Pennsylvania 18431
ISBN: 978-1-62979-950-6
Manufactured in Shenzhen, Guangdong, China
Mfg. 10/2019
First edition
Visit our website at Highlights.com.
10 9 8 7 6 5 4 3 2 1